Big Cats

Claire Llewellyn

KINGFISHER

NEW YORK

KINGFISHER
LONDON & NEW YORK

Copyright © Kingfisher 2013
Published in the United States by Kingfisher,
175 Fifth Ave., New York, NY 10010
Kingfisher is an imprint of Macmillan Children's Books, London.
All rights reserved.

Illustrations by: Peter Bull Art Studio

Distributed in the U.S. and Canada by Macmillan,
175 Fifth Ave., New York, NY 10010

Library of Congress Cataloging-in-Publication data
has been applied for.

ISBN: 978-0-7534-6743-5

Kingfisher books are available for special promotions and
premiums. For details contact: Special Markets Department,
Macmillan, 175 Fifth Ave., New York, NY 10010.

For more information, please visit
www.kingfisherbooks.com

Printed in China

1 3 5 7 9 8 6 4 2

1TR/0912/UTD/WKT/140MA

Picture credits

**The Publisher would like to thank the following
for permission to reproduce their material.
(t = top, b = bottom, c = center, l = left, r = right):**
Pages 4 Naturepl/Tony Heald; 5tl Shutterstock/Eric Isselee; 5tr
Shutterstock/palko72; 5cl Corbis/Tom Brakefield; 5cr Corbis/
Roger Wood; 5bc Samantha Richiardi; 6 Shutterstock/Nagel
Photography; 8c Photolibrary/Oxford Scientific Films (OSF); 8bl
Shutterstock/Heather McCann; 9tl Getty/Karine Aigner/National
Geographic; 9tr Photolibrary/Bios; 9cr Photoshot/NHPA; 9bl
Shutterstock/pixelparticle; 10 Shutterstock/Mirek Srb; 12cl
Photoshot/NHPA; 12cr Photolibrary/Index Stock Imagery; 13tl
Photolibrary/Peter Arnold Images; 13tr Corbis/Daniel J. Cox;
13cr Photolibrary/OSF; 13bl Getty/Martin Harvey/Gallo Images;
13br Corbis/Daniel J. Cox; 14 Shutterstock/EcoPrint; 16tl Naturepl/
Richard du Toit; 16cr Frank Lane Picture Agency (FLPA)/Winfried
Wisniewski; 16cl Photoshot/NHPA; 17tl Naturepl/Susi Eszterhas;
17tr Ardea/Thomas Marent; 17bl FLPA/Rob Reijnen/Minden; 17br
FLPA/Jurgen & Christine Sohns; 18 Shutterstock/photobar; 20bl
Alamy/Mike Hill; 21tl Photolibrary/Superstock; 21tr FLPA/Pete
Oxford/Minden; 21c Naturepl/Carine Schrurs; 21bl Naturepl/
Anup Shah; 21br FLPA/David Hosking; 22 FLPA/Richard du
Toit/Minden; 24cl FLPA/Michael Krebs/Imagebroker; 24cr Getty/
Anup Shah/The Image Bank; 24bl FLPA/Suzi Eszterhas/Minden;
24br Getty/Panoramic Images; 25t FLPA/Photo Researchers;
25b FLPA/Richard du Toit/Minden; 26 FLPA/Michael Durham/
Minden; 28cr Corbis/Zhang Xiaoli/Xinhua Press; 28b FLPA/Fritz
Polking; 29l Naturepl/Luiz Claudio Marigo; 29tc Corbis/Alexandra
Boulat; 29tr Naturepl/Andy Rouse; 29br Alamy/Purestock;
30tr FLPA/Elliot Neep; 30ctl Shutterstock/Stephen Meese;
30cbl Shutterstock/Andy Poole; 30cbr FLPA/Terry Whitaker;
30bl Photolibrary/Bios; 30br Photolibrary/David Painter;
31tr Shutterstock/Cheryl Ann Quigley; 31ctl Shutterstock/Galyna
Andrushko; 31ctr Alamy/Arco Images; 31bl Photolibrary/Peter
Arnold Images; 31br Shutterstock/EcoPrint.

Contents

More to explore

On some of the pages in this book, you will find colored buttons with symbols on them. There are four different colors, and each one belongs to a different topic. Choose a topic, follow its colored buttons through the book, and you'll make some interesting discoveries of your own.

For example, on page 6 you'll find a green button, like this, next to a wetland scene. The green buttons are about places around the world where big cats live.

Page 27

World

There is a page number in the button. Turn to that page (page 27) to find a green button on another place where big cats live. Follow all the steps through the book, and at the end of your journey you'll find out how the steps are linked and discover even more information about this topic.

Cat cousins

Record breakers

Prey animals

The other topics in this book are cat cousins, record breakers, and prey animals. Follow the steps and see what you can discover!

What are big cats?

Lions, tigers, leopards, and jaguars are all big cats. These animals are powerful hunters with sharp claws and teeth. Some big cats live in tropical areas, but others are found in cooler places. Many have been hunted for their fur and are now endangered.

Adult male lions have a shaggy mane.

The African lion is one of the world's best hunters. Big cats are carnivores—they eat only meat, and they first have to catch it. They are strong, stealthy, and have plenty of weapons to kill their prey.

plenty of muscle

sharp teeth and strong jaws

a hungry lion on the prowl

long, fast legs

powerful paws

sharp claws

Big cats have beautiful fur coats.

A long-legged serval rests on the grass.

a jaguar's coat

a tigress with her three cubs

The serval is one of about 35 smaller wild cats. Others include the ocelot and the lynx. Wild cats are related to big cats, but unlike their larger cousins, they cannot roar.

The ancient Egyptians made beautiful statues of cats.

A female tiger feeds and protects her young until they can take care of themselves. Big cats are mammals. Baby cubs grow inside their mother's body for about three months. Then she gives birth to them and feeds them on her milk.

Pet cats belong to the same family as wild cats. Cats first lived with people 5,000 years ago. They guarded supplies of food from mice. Now cats are our companions.

The perfect cat

Every part of a cat's body helps it move, hunt, and survive. Strong muscles make it fast and agile. Sharp senses—sight, hearing, and smell—alert it to food or danger. The cat's size and power and its jaws and claws help it catch prey.

What is this?

Page 27

1. A pair of green iguanas climb up a tree.

2. A black howler monkey calls the alarm.

3. A hyacinth macaw flies away, squawking.

? This is a peccary's snout. Peccaries look like wild pigs and are prey for jaguars.

Page 22

In the wetlands of Brazil, a jaguar pounces on a caiman lurking in the water. The caiman has little chance of escape. Jaguars are at home in water. They are strong swimmers with muscular bodies and a powerful bite. Nearby animals call out warnings and hurry away.

Page 15

4 A startled stork makes its escape.

5 Wetlands are made up of marshes and pools.

6 Caimans are alligators that live in fresh water.

Amazing bodies

Big cats are some of the world's most agile animals. Powerful and beautiful, they can run, leap, pounce, stalk, climb, and swim. From their sharp eyes and ears to their long, strong tail, every part of their body has adapted for survival in the wild.

Long, bendy spine can flex and stretch.

Long tail helps the body balance.

Strong muscles power the lightweight frame.

A cheetah has a long supple spine (backbone) that allows it to stretch its long legs to the limit. In a life-or-death chase after its prey, the cheetah can cover 23 ft. (7m) in a single bound.

soft pads under the paws help with silent stalking.

a lion cub's paw

The lynx figures out the world around it using superb senses. Forward-facing eyes judge distances well. Long ears turn to pick up every rustle. Stiff, sensitive whiskers help the cat judge gaps and spaces, and to feel its way.

sharp, curved claws grip prey and help with climbing.

The margay spends most of its life in the trees. It is an acrobatic climber. Its broad feet, flexible toes, and strong claws help give it a good grip. Its long tail helps it balance.

A margay climbs down head first.

A leopard stays fully alert while it drinks at a watering hole at night. Its eyes have a shiny backing, which boosts the light of the moon and stars, helping the cat see in the dark.

Eyes catch the light and seem to glow.

Page 22

What is this?

1 Snow leopards may hunt in pairs.

2 Smoky-gray fur blends in with the rocky. snowy ground.

3 Large paws work like snowshoes.

Habitat for a cat

The place where an animal lives is called its habitat. Big cats live in many different habitats. Some live in tropical forests. Others need grassy plains or rocky mountains. Wherever an animal lives, its habitat provides it with food and shelter and space to hunt and roam.

Page 30

Page 19

In the harsh mountains of Central Asia, two young snow leopards are hunting. Teaming up gives them a greater chance of success. Strong and sure-footed, they leap over a ravine to chase game birds in the snow. Their long tails help them balance. Higher up, wild sheep graze on scrubby grass. They, too, are a snow leopard's prey.

This is a snow leopard's nose. The large nostrils help suck in more of the thin mountain air.

All sorts of homes

Deserts, forests, mountains, marshes—big cats are found in a wide range of places. Most species live in a particular habitat. Over thousands of years, they have developed skills and features that help them survive in their home landscape and climate.

Caracals live in dry scrub. They survive on little water.

A sandy coat blends in with the background.

The Siberian tiger is found in the **mountain forests** of southeast Russia. It lives farther north than any other kind of tiger. Its large size and thick fur help it survive winter temperatures of −49°F (−45°C).

at home in
the desert

The **cougar**, also known as the puma and the mountain lion, has adapted to many different habitats. It is found in forests, deserts, wetlands, and mountains in North and South America.

Panthers are excellent climbers and are at home in the trees. This one is a black leopard in a **tropical forest** in Africa. Black-coated jaguars in the Amazon rainforest are also called panthers.

Cougars have even been seen in towns.

a serval stalking water rats

at home in the mountains

Servals hunt in **marshes and lakes**. Their long ears help them hunt, pinpointing the rustles of rats, birds, and frogs hidden in the reeds.

What is this?

1 African wild dogs may try to steal the kill.

2 The approaching lions stay low.

3 Each lion is just a short sprint away from its prey.

Page 30

Hunting together

A pride of lions lives together and hunts together, too. A group of them will stalk and attack their prey and then share the kill with the others. Teamwork helps lions hunt animals much bigger than themselves. Other big cats cannot do this because they hunt alone.

④ Two young males join in the hunt.

⑤ Cape buffalo are bulky and fierce and can scare away lions.

⑥ Most hunting starts at dusk, as the light fades.

15

⑥

⑤

Page 26

Page 11

On the grasslands of Africa, a group of lionesses are stalking buffalo. The cats grunt softly to one another, inching forward into the breeze so that their scent will not carry to their prey. They crouch down low to stay hidden. One of them spots a weaker animal and suddenly sprints toward it. The others move in to help with the kill.

↻ This is a buffalo's long, curving horn. The sharp horns are dangerous and can injure lions.

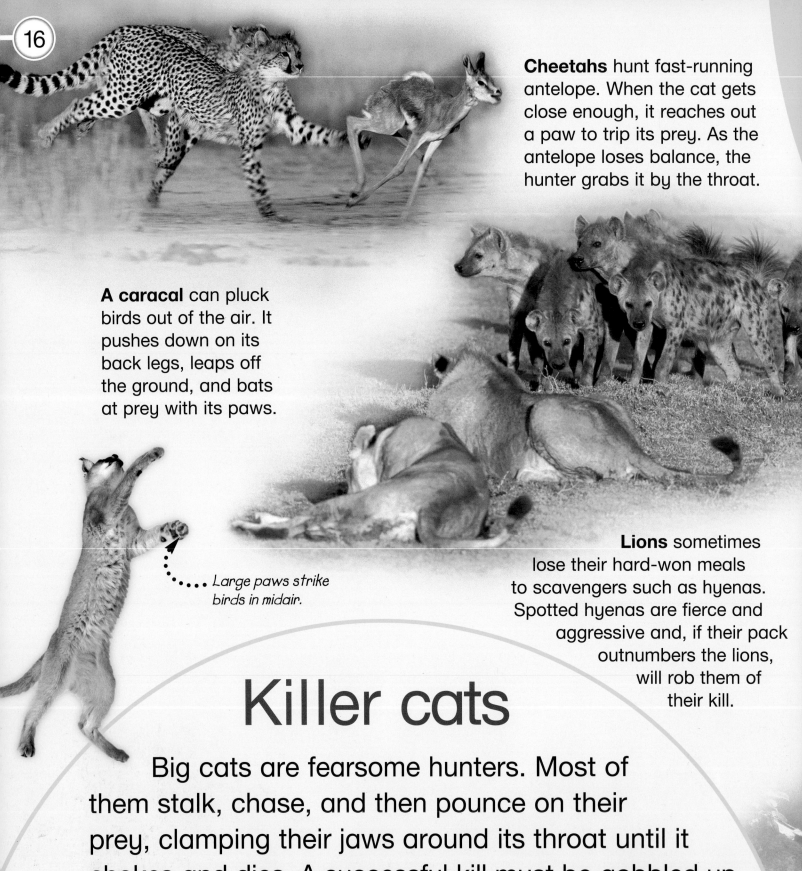

Cheetahs hunt fast-running antelope. When the cat gets close enough, it reaches out a paw to trip its prey. As the antelope loses balance, the hunter grabs it by the throat.

A caracal can pluck birds out of the air. It pushes down on its back legs, leaps off the ground, and bats at prey with its paws.

Large paws strike birds in midair.

Lions sometimes lose their hard-won meals to scavengers such as hyenas. Spotted hyenas are fierce and aggressive and, if their pack outnumbers the lions, will rob them of their kill.

Killer cats

Big cats are fearsome hunters. Most of them stalk, chase, and then pounce on their prey, clamping their jaws around its throat until it chokes and dies. A successful kill must be gobbled up fast, or it may be stolen by scavengers—meat eaters, such as hyenas or vultures, that feed on animal remains.

A lioness and her cub suck and crunch zebra bones.

a mess of juicy meat and bone

Back teeth crack bones and slice meat.

Long, sharp fangs stab and tear.

Small front teeth nibble flesh from the bone.

A leopard quickly protects its kill before other animals can smell it. The cat drags the carcass into a tree, where scavengers cannot follow.

A leopard carries its kill in its mouth.

The jaguar has the most powerful bite of any cat. Unlike other big cats, it kills its prey not by suffocation but by biting right through the skull. It then uses its teeth to open the carcass and tear meat from the bones.

Cats have a rough tongue to lick bones clean.

Cat fights

Big cats live in different ways. Most species live alone, but young male cheetahs stay together, often for their entire lives. They find a hunting ground with food, water, and females for breeding. They guard this territory from other cheetahs and will fight to the death to defend it.

What are these?

Page 14

① Two male cheetahs stand their ground.

② Cats flatten their ears when angry or afraid.

③ Gemsbok antelope graze on the scrub.

? These are a cheetah's bared teeth. The row of sharp, white teeth makes the cat look more threatening.

On their hunting ground in the Kalahari Desert in Africa, two cheetahs meet an intruder. It is another male, hungry and hunting for food. The angry cats glare at it, crouching low and growling. The stranger understands the signs and the choice before it. It can fight and maybe get hurt—or turn around and leave.

3

Page 30

4

5

6

4 A solo male is looking for territory.

5 Cats crouch low when they are ready to attack.

6 Grasses and thorny shrubs grow in the red sand.

Getting along

Most big cats live alone. Individuals from the same species spread out to avoid competing for prey. They communicate with one another across large distances, using sound, scent, and visual signs to get their message across.

Most lions roar at dawn and dusk.

An adult male lion roars loudly to keep other lions off its patch. Big cats tend to keep out of one another's way. It helps them avoid fights and life-threatening injuries.

When a **female jaguar** is ready to mate, she broadcasts the news around the forest with loud calls and special scent markings. These help males within her range track her down.

male jaguar

female jaguar

a snow leopard hunting for a meal

Lions are the only big cats to live in groups. Most prides are made up of about 15 animals—one or two males, five or six females, and a handful of youngsters and cubs.

A snow leopard spends most of its life alone, except during the breeding season. Prey can be scarce in the mountains, so adults need a large territory to help them survive.

A female tiger signals to males by spraying her scent on a tree.

A caracal scratches a tree with its claws. The marks are a sign for others to see. They say, "Trespassers, keep out! This territory is taken!"

What is this?

1. These cubs are six to seven weeks old.

2. Play-fighting helps the cubs grow stronger.

3. Eagles could attack young cubs.

Page 15

Page 18

Mother and cubs

Before a female cat gives birth, she has to find a den, such as an old burrow or a thick bush. Here, her cubs are hidden from danger and sheltered from the weather. The mother feeds and raises the cubs on her own. She has to leave them behind in the den when she goes out hunting.

4 A hollow by a fallen tree trunk makes a good den.

5 A cub purrs loudly as it is washed.

6 A leopard's paw print is called a pug.

Page 11

Four leopard cubs relax outside the den where they were born. Their mother is washing one of them. Two more are play-fighting with each other, practicing skills they will soon need for hunting. The female leopard stays alert. She will move the cubs back inside the den if she senses danger.

This is the mother leopard's tongue. Its rough texture helps clean the cubs' fur.

Family life

Raising a litter is hard work. From the moment her tiny cubs are born, a mother cat feeds and protects them. They may be with her for more than two years. She will teach them everything she knows about hunting and survival.

A lynx mother cleans her newborn cub.

......*Newborn cubs are blind and helpless.*

A lioness carries a cub in her mouth while two more follow alongside. Big cats use their teeth very gently to grasp the loose skin at the back of their cub's neck.

A cheetah feeds her nine-day-old cubs. For the first weeks, cubs feed only on milk. The mother must eat meat so that her body can produce nourishing milk. She leaves her babies while she hunts.

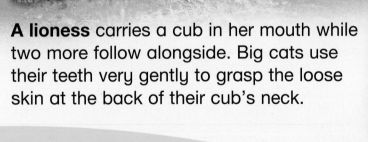

A cheetah cub eats meat caught by its mother.

The cub is eight weeks old.

Young cubs learn as they play. Bigger cubs often "hunt" one another—learning to climb, balance, stalk, and pounce. They do not bite for real, and they keep their sharp claws in—most of the time!

Tiger cubs spend a lot of time playing.

The cub in front makes a clumsy attempt to pounce.

Cheetah cubs begin to learn to hunt from the age of about 12 weeks. Their mother brings home live prey so that they can practice how to kill.

Saving big cats

Tigers and other big cats face a difficult future. In our crowded world, there is less space for them to hunt and breed. Hungry tigers attack farm animals and, sometimes, humans, too. Just a few thousand tigers live in the wild. If we do not help them fast, they could become extinct.

Page 30

1

2

3

What is this?

?

1 Walkie-talkies help forest workers stay in touch.

2 The tiger has been drugged.

3 The collar tracks the tiger using satellite technology.

? This is a tiger's footprint. Each tiger has its own unique prints, which can be used to identify it.

4

6

Page 23

5

In a rainforest in India, a Bengal tiger sleeps on the ground. Conservation workers have tranquillized the animal so that they can put on a special collar. One worker attaches a camera to a tree. The collar and camera will track the tiger's movements— helping keep it away from humans and out of harm's way.

4 The workers use a jeep to travel through the forest.

5 This gun was used to fire the tranquillizer dart.

6 Camera traps provide information about tigers.

People and big cats

Humans harm big cats. We destroy their habitat, hunt their prey, and some people even kill them for their skins. Yet humans also help big cats. Scientists study them, while others set up reserves where cats can live safely.

A female leopard watches **farmers**' cows. Big cats often go hungry as people take over their habitats and hunt their prey. Yet if they attack people's livestock, the cats will probably be shot.

Big cats are still used in circuses in some parts of the world.

A leopard watches Masai herders and their cattle in Kenya.

Cats lose their habitat when forests are destroyed.

Tourists pay to see big cats in the wild. The money pays for conservation work. It also helps support locals and discourage them from hunting.

People build homes or farms on the cleared land.

Zoos study and breed big cats. They also inspire and educate visitors and help raise funds for conservation work overseas.

The fur trade is a serious threat to big cats. Each year, thousands of animals are hunted for their fur, even though this is illegal. This official has seized jaguar skins from a criminal gang.

The snow leopard is a **long-jump champion**. It has been known to cross ravines 46 ft. (14m) wide—ten times the length of its own body!

snow leopard

At less than 130 lb. (60kg), leopards are the smallest big cats. Yet they are the **strongest climbers**. An adult male can drag a carcass three times its own weight up a tree.

Record breakers

Jaguars live in Central and South America, mostly in the Amazon rainforest. There are only about 15,000 of them left in the wild.

Tigers live in Asia, in areas dotted from China to the far east of Russia. There are about 3,500 tigers left in the wild.

World

The wetlands of Brazil are home to **ocelots** as well as jaguars. They are smaller than jaguars and hunt smaller prey, such as fish, crabs, turtles, and lizards. Like jaguars, they are hunted for their beautiful fur.

Leopards sometimes hunt the **African golden cat**. This cat lives in thick scrubland and forests and hunts at night.

Cat cousins

The Yacaré caiman looks like a small alligator. It lives in fresh water in the wetlands and rainforests of South America. It feeds on snails, snakes, piranhas, and other fish.

caiman

Cape buffalo live in herds of more than 1,000 animals. They graze on grass at night and rest during the day. If a buffalo is attacked, the other animals in the herd rush to its defense.

Prey animals

More to explore

Cheetahs are the **fastest animals** on land, reaching a top speed of 68 mph (110km/h) in less than four seconds. Large nostrils and lungs supply them with all the oxygen they need during these sudden bursts of energy.

paws like running shoes

a leopard in scrubby grassland, Africa

Lions, tigers, leopards, and jaguars are the only cats that can roar. Of these, the lion is the **loudest,** with a roar that can be heard more than 5 mi. (8km) away.

Leopards cover the largest range of any wild cat—from central and east Africa to India, Southeast Asia, and China. They are doing well in Africa, but elsewhere their numbers are falling.

Snow leopards live in the mountains of central Asia. Their range covers an area the size of Greenland, but this is spread over 12 countries. There are fewer than 7,000 snow leopards left in the wild.

Africa's grasslands are famous for lions, but medium-size cats called **caracals** live there, too. They have sharp hearing and are so fast that they can catch antelope and hares.

large ears

In the same forests as tigers, **clouded leopards** live and hunt. These medium-size cats are excellent climbers. They prey on monkeys, porcupines, and deer.

chukor partridge

Chukor partridges live in small flocks on rocky hillsides throughout Asia. The birds feed on seeds, roots, and ants. In the winter, they move to the shelter of the lower slopes.

A gemsbok is a kind of antelope with spearlike horns. It feeds on herbs, grasses, shrubs, and roots. It is well adapted to desert life and can survive for weeks without water.

Index